Our World

VOLCANOES AND EARTHQUAKES

Basil Booth

Titles in this series

Coasts

Deserts

The Earth in Space

Grasslands

Jungles and Rainforests

Mountains

Polar Regions

Pollution and Conservation

Rivers and Lakes

Rocks, Minerals and Fossils

Seas and Oceans

Temperate Forests

Volcanoes and Earthquakes

Weather and Climate

First published in 1988 by
Wayland (Publishers) Ltd
61 Western Road, Hove
East Sussex BN3 1JD

© Copyright Wayland (Publishers) Ltd

Edited by Jollands Editions
Series design by Malcolm Smythe
Book design by Malcolm Walker

British Library Cataloguing in Publication Data
Booth, Basil
   Volcanoes and Earthquakes
   1. Earthquakes and volcanoes for schools.
   I. Title   II. Series
   551.2
   ISBN 1–85210–605–0

Typeset by DP Press, Sevenoaks, Kent
Printed in Italy by G. Canale & C.S.p.A., Turin.
Bound in Belgium by Casterman S.A.

Front cover, main picture A night eruption of Kilauea – Iki in Hawaii, 1959.

Front cover, inset Earthquake damage in Anchorage, Alaska, in 1964.

Back cover Hot springs in New Zealand.

Contents

What are volcanoes?

Volcanoes are openings in the surface of the earth, from which molten rock and gas escape. Volcanoes may erupt either from fissures, which are large cracks in the earth's crust, or from vents, which are tube-like holes.

The 'smoke' that volcanoes give off is really made up of ash, cinder and larger pieces of rock called blocks and bombs. All these products are thrown out of the volcano by the escaping gases and pile up around the vent to give the familiar shaped cone.

Not all volcanoes have elegant cones like those of Mt Fujiyama in Japan, or El Teide in Tenerife. Some are simply long cracks in the ground which release red-hot lava flows. These can devastate large areas of countryside. Such eruptions are common on Hawaii and, to a lesser extent, Iceland. Some volcanoes have no cone at all; innocent looking circular lakes like Laziale and Bolzena, in Italy, are really large volcanic craters filled with water. These volcanoes have rest periods ranging from 10,000 to 20,000 years, while they lie dormant between explosive eruptions of devastating violence. If these volcanoes were to erupt today they could wipe out the city of Rome overnight.

Volcanoes are usually classified as active, dormant or extinct. This traditional system is based on whether or not a volcano has erupted in historic times, or is releasing volcanic gas through fumaroles, which are holes in the ground. The main problem with this system of classification is that historic time varies greatly from one part of the world to another. For example, the history of Mt Etna, in Italy, started nearly 3,500 years ago, while records for Mt Lamington, in New Guinea, total only 37 years. Mt Lamington's wooded slopes hid a killer that erupted in 1951, causing 3,000 deaths.

Left Trees and bushes burn as a crack opens across a road, releasing fluid runny lava and fire fountains during the 1969 eruption of Kilauea, a live active volcano on Hawaii.

Right The massive El Teide volcano, in Tenerife, rises above the clouds to 3781 m. A live but dormant volcano, it has produced eruptions of enormous violence during the past 32,000 years.

Far Right A prehistoric eruption produced the large caldera which contains this 200 m high parasol cone on Bromo volcano, Indonesia. The 2329 m high volcano is live, though dormant.

Lava flows and fire fountains are typical of volcanic activity on Mt Etna, Italy, seen here erupting in 1973.

In 1979, a UNESCO (United Nations Educational, Scientific and Cultural Organization) meeting of world volcanologists decided upon a new classification scheme for volcanoes. Those that may erupt in the future are now called live, and those which may not erupt are now called dead. When live volcanoes are erupting they are referred to as active and when they are not they are dormant.

Famous volcanoes

The largest volcanic event in history took place in 1883, when the island of Krakatoa, in Indonesia, vanished during a violently explosive eruption.

It is generally supposed that the huge explosions were caused by sea water pouring into the red-hot magma chamber. However, if this had happened the island would have blown up and scattered rock fragments along the coasts of neighbouring Java and Sumatra. The volcanic deposits on these coasts contain only fine ash and pumice, and no large fragments of Krakatoa island. This suggests that Krakatoa did not actually 'blow up'.

The island volcano disappeared by slowly sinking into its own magma chamber as it emptied its contents high into the atmosphere. The huge explosions were caused by massive flows of gas and red-hot rock fragments entering the sea and cooling instantly as they came into contact with the cold water. These explosions were responsible for creating the giant tidal waves, or tsunamis, that caused the enormous loss of life along the coasts of the nearby islands.

The summits of many big volcanoes have large, circular hollows called calderas. These vary greatly in size; for example, the caldera of Tambora, in Sumatra, is 6 km in diameter; the Valles caldera, in New Mexico, is 23 km across and the one in the Long Valley of California, USA, is 16 km by 30 km.

Volcanoes with huge calderas have produced some of the biggest eruptions known on earth. Even the 1883 event of Krakatoa is small compared with one that took place on Tenerife in the Canary Islands, 32,000 years ago.

Lava eruptions are not so famous as explosive events. However, in 1783, Iceland lost one fifth of its population as a result of the Laki fissure eruption. So much gas and volcanic dust was produced that it caused a mini ice age in Europe that year by shutting out the sun, so preventing the winter snows from melting.

Above Steam and gas pour from a new vent on the sea floor during the birth of the Surtsey volcano off Iceland.

Right The beginning of the blast that ripped the side out of Mt St. Helens, USA, in 1980.

Left Pompeii, in Italy, was destroyed by the massive eruption of Mt Vesuvius in AD 79. It was rediscovered in 1711 and is now well preserved.

What are earthquakes?

Earthquakes are severe shocks that are caused when intense vibrations pass through solid rock. The vibrations are produced when rocks below the surface break suddenly along faults, which are giant cracks that may run for many kilometres across, or below, the earth's surface. Faults relieve the strain that builds up on the plates that make up the outer crust of our planet. The plates are slowly pushed about the face of the earth by convection currents, deep below the surface.

When a rock fractures, shock waves are produced in much the same way as when a piece of wood is snapped. The passage of these shock waves through the crust causes the ground to crack and break up, buildings to topple, rivers to overflow and giant waves to be produced at sea. Some quakes last only for a few minutes, while others continue for several days, though not continuously. In 1966, an earthquake in Tashkent, USSR, lasted for 38 days. It destroyed 39,000 homes and killed 18 people.

Earthquake intensity is measured in several ways. One method is the Mercalli Scale, which describes what is felt or seen by the people who witness an earthquake. This scale varies from small vibrations that cause ornaments to fall off shelves, to large shocks that cause the ground to move up and down in waves, and large cracks to appear. There are three such scales which can give valuable information about quakes in areas where expensive seismograms are not available.

Seismograms measure the actual intensity of an earthquake, providing data that can be used to calculate the total energy released. The Richter Scale is used to show this energy. An increase of one unit on the scale means the quake is 30–35 times more powerful than the one below it. There is no upper limit, but few quakes exceed 8.0.

The number of earthquakes occuring each year is probably in excess of several thousand, though most can be detected only with sensitive instruments. Only twenty to thirty are large enough to rank as disastrous events.

Houses collapsed as the ground rose and sank during the 1964 earthquake at Anchorage, Alaska.

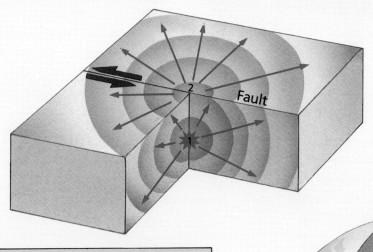

Left Movement on a fault creates an earthquake at the focus (1). Shock waves spread out hitting the surface at the epicentre (2).

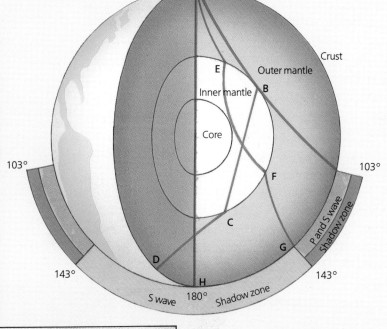

Above Earthquake waves do not travel in straight lines through the earth. Their paths are curved and they are refracted, or bent, at mantle boundaries. Often they are refracted twice. This means in some areas, called shadow zones, the shocks cannot be recorded.

Left San Francisco, USA, lies in ruins after the disastrous earthquake and fire of 1906.

Famous earthquakes

At 5.30 pm on 27 March 1964, an earthquake measuring 8.9 on the Richter Scale struck Prince William Sound in Alaska, USA.

The earthquake lasted for four minutes, during which time the shocks set off avalanches and landslides throughout south and central Alaska. In Anchorage, 160 km from the epicentre (the point above the centre of the earthquake), buildings rocked to and fro, while large cracks opened in the ground and swallowed objects as large as cars. On Turn Again Heights, the whole area slid more than 500 m, carrying away homes amidst a jumbled mass of soil, telegraph poles and trees. On Alaska's coasts, 8 m high tsunamis created havoc, while 4360 km away, 6 m waves caused severe damage along California's beaches. Some 200,000 sq km of countryside was raised or dropped by this event, which killed 114 people.

At 5.13 am on 18 April 1906, a severe earthquake on the San Andreas Fault struck the city of San Francisco, USA. The quake lasted barely a minute, but during this time it reduced the city to ruins. It caused $1,000 million of damage and killed 700 people.

In terms of death toll, the San Francisco quake was a very minor event, for on 23 January 1556, between half a million and one million people were killed in the Shensi Province, China, when it was struck by the worst known quake in history.

A selection of the most disastrous earthquakes of the last one hundred years

Year	Place	Estimated casualties
1891	Mino-Owari, Japan	7,300
1896	Sanriku, Japan	27,000
1905	Kangra, India	19,000
1908	Messina, Sicily	160,000
1915	Avezzano, Italy	30,000
1920	Kansu, China	200,000
1923	Tokyo and Yokohama, Japan	143,000
1932	Kansu, China	70,000
1935	Quetta, Baluchistan	60,000
1939	Concepcion, Chile	30,000
1939	Erzincan, Turkey	40,000
1944	San Juan, Argentina	5,000
1948	Fuki, Japan	5,000
1949	Ambato, Ecuador	6,000
1949	Tadzhikistan, USSR	10,000
1960	Southern Chile	5,700
1960	Agadir, Morocco	14,000
1962	Northwestern Iran	14,000
1970	Peru	60,000
1972	Managua, Nicaragua	10,000
1972	Jahrom, Iran	5,044
1976	Guatemala	20,000
1976	Tientsin (Tangshan), China	650,000
1976	Mindanao, Philippines	8,000
1976	Eastern Turkey	5-10,000
1978	Tabas, Iran	15,000

Ruins of Lisbon, Portugal, after the earthquake of 1755 which killed 10–15,000 people.

Most of the deaths were caused by the collapse of homes which were built into the hillsides, and by drowning in the tremendous floods as rivers burst their banks. The disease and famine that followed caused still further deaths and suffering.

Since then, China has suffered from many disastrous earthquakes. In 1976, a quake measuring 7.2 on the Richter Scale, the largest since the Alaska event of 1964, hit the Tiensin Province causing tremendous damage and killing over 650,000 people. The full figures are yet to be announced by the Chinese government, but it is thought that the total could exceed that of 1556. This would make it the worst recorded earthquake disaster in history.

Right Japan is notorious for its earthquakes. Here, the Nihombushi district of Tokyo lies in ruins after the devastating earthquake of 1923 in which 143,000 people died.

Left Survivors wander through the ruins of Messina in Sicily, Italy, after the great earthquake of 1908 which killed 160,000 people.

Where do volcanoes occur?

Volcanoes occur along lines of weakness in the earth's crust, where the plates that make up the ocean floor meet one another.

These plate margins, or boundaries, include constructive plate margins, where plates are being created, and destructive plate margins, where plates are being destroyed. Plates are destroyed when the edge of a plate is forced into a deep trench, and eventually into the molten layers below. Volcanoes occur also where a mantle plume, a 'hot-spot', melts a hole in the overlying plate.

The best known volcanic zones occur on the destructive plate margins around the Pacific Ring of Fire. This is made up of a chain of volcanoes that lie along the west coast of South and Central America, through the Aleutian Islands to the north, Japan and the Philippines, across New Zealand and into the Antarctic.

Other volcanoes occur in mid-ocean, along the line of ocean ridges. Ocean ridges are submerged mountain ranges where the ocean floor spreads apart and molten rock pushes up from below. The Mid-Atlantic Ridge and the East Pacific Rise are two examples of ocean floor volcanism. In places, underwater volcanoes have grown to form islands such as the Azores, Ascension Island and Tristan da Cunha.

Some volcanoes occur away from these lines of weakness, where they have forced holes through the middle of a plate. These include the Hawaiian volcanoes, which have punched holes through the centre of the Pacific Oceanic Plate, and some African volcanoes, which have risen through the middle of a much thicker, continental plate.

The Smithsonian Institute, of the USA, lists 1,343 volcanoes which have erupted over the past 10,000 years. This figure does not include those volcanoes that occur on ocean floors, or those that erupt less than once every 10,000 years. The correct figure will probably never be known, but it could be nearer 12,000.

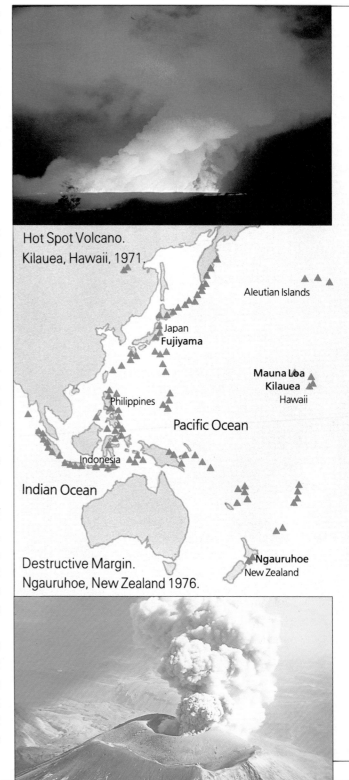

Hot Spot Volcano.
Kilauea, Hawaii, 1971.

Aleutian Islands

Japan
Fujiyama

**Mauna Loa
Kilauea**
Hawaii

Philippines

Pacific Ocean

Indonesia

Indian Ocean

Destructive Margin.
Ngauruhoe, New Zealand 1976.

Ngauruhoe
New Zealand

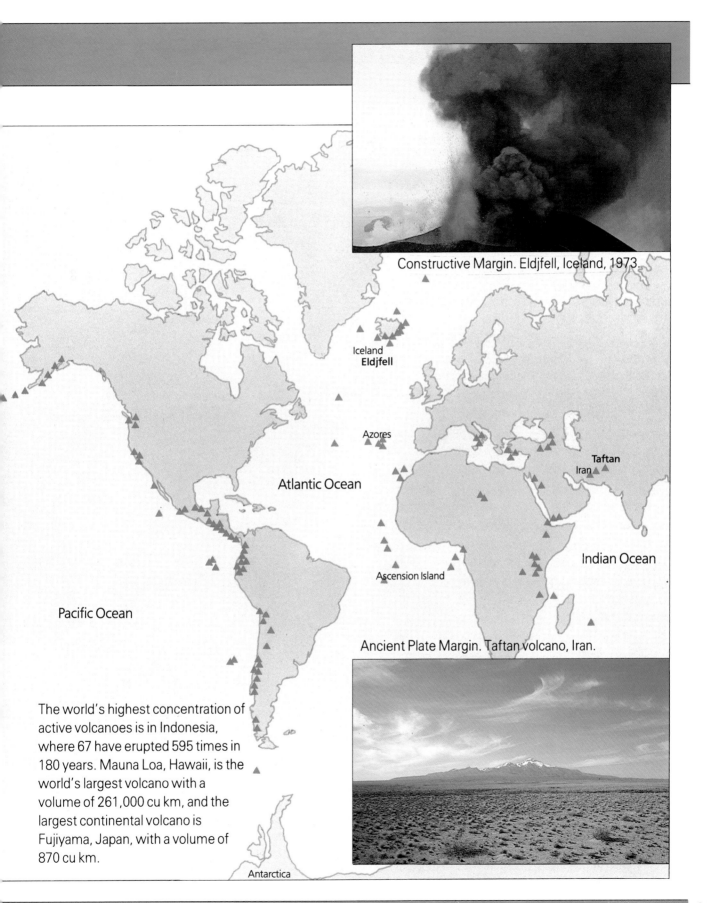

Constructive Margin. Eldjfell, Iceland, 1973.

Iceland
Eldjfell

Azores

Taftan
Iran

Atlantic Ocean

Indian Ocean

Ascension Island

Pacific Ocean

Ancient Plate Margin. Taftan volcano, Iran.

The world's highest concentration of active volcanoes is in Indonesia, where 67 have erupted 595 times in 180 years. Mauna Loa, Hawaii, is the world's largest volcano with a volume of 261,000 cu km, and the largest continental volcano is Fujiyama, Japan, with a volume of 870 cu km.

Antarctica

Where do earthquakes occur?

There are two types of earthquakes: shallow ones that take place in the thin outer layer of the earth's crust, and deep ones that occur at depths of up to 800 km, in the lower part of the upper mantle.

Most of the shallow quakes take place on transform faults that cut across spreading plate margins like the Mid-Atlantic Ridge. The deeper quakes are produced below the trenches where plates are being destroyed. These are found beneath continents like South America and under island arcs, which are curved chains of islands, such as Indonesia. Because of this, earthquakes occur mostly in the same zones as volcanoes.

While earthquakes do not produce volcanoes, volcanoes do generate earthquakes. These are of such low intensity that damage is caused only rarely. Some of the largest and most disastrous quakes take place in areas like Central America, Japan, China, India and Alaska. China and India lie neither on constructive or destructive plate margins. However, they do have great mountain chains running across them, along ancient continental collision boundaries. The mountains are still growing and they are under great enough stresses to cause them to fracture and produce earthquakes.

One such collision zone runs across the tip of North Africa, through the Mediterranean, Turkey, Iran and into the Himalayas of northern India. The movement along this collision zone causes earthquakes in Morocco, southern Italy, Turkey and Afghanistan.

Where movement between plates takes place continuously, tiny earthquakes are being produced all the time. When this movement stops, the forces that are causing it continue to build up, creating enormous stress where the two plates join. Eventually the stress exceeds the strength of the rocks, which snap, sending out the severe shock waves that cause so much damage.

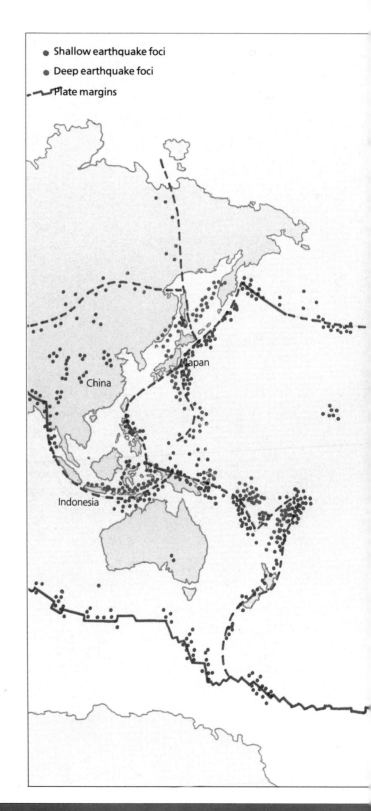

- Shallow earthquake foci
- Deep earthquake foci
- - Plate margins

China

Japan

Indonesia

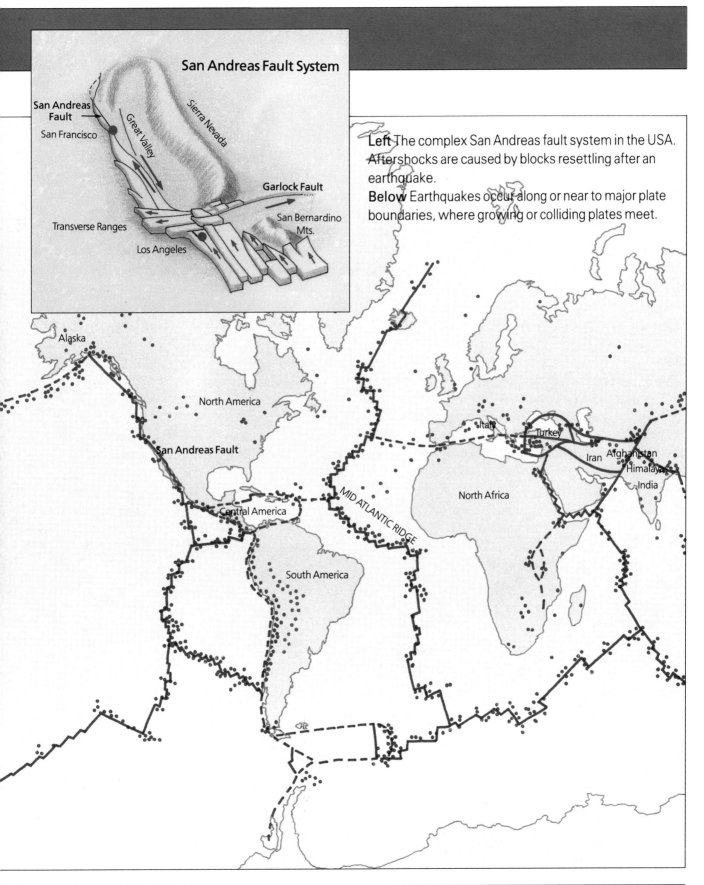

San Andreas Fault System

San Andreas Fault

San Francisco

Great Valley

Sierra Nevada

Transverse Ranges

Los Angeles

Garlock Fault

San Bernardino Mts.

Left The complex San Andreas fault system in the USA. Aftershocks are caused by blocks resettling after an earthquake.
Below Earthquakes occur along or near to major plate boundaries, where growing or colliding plates meet.

Alaska

North America

San Andreas Fault

Central America

MID ATLANTIC RIDGE

South America

Italy

Turkey

Iran

Afghanistan

Himalayas

India

North Africa

Moving plates

Nearly 60 years ago a German scientist died amidst the frozen wastes of the Greenland ice-cap. The scientist, Alfred Wegener, was thought by many to be a crank. His theories were rejected because he suggested that the continents moved about the face of the earth. Today, we know that he was right.

It was Professor Hess of Princeton University, USA, who found that ocean floors were moving slowly away from oceanic ridges. Some move as much as 8 cm in one year, which is fast by geological standards. As they move apart, new ocean floor is created from molten rock which rises from deep in the mantle. As a result, the rocks either side of a ridge are very young, but they increase in age the further they are from the ridge.

The dating of volcanic rocks was made possible by the discoveries of scientists working in Cambridge University, England, under Sir Edward Bullard. They found that the earth's magnetic field had reversed regularly throughout its history. When this happens, the south magnetic pole becomes the north magnetic pole and vice versa. When magma cools it becomes imprinted with the earth's magnetic field of the time and this helps with the dating.

By 1969 the theory of plate tectonics was born. The theory explained how new ocean floor was created at oceanic ridges (spreading plate margins) and destroyed in the deep oceanic trenches that border continents (destructive plate margins). Stretching out from the spreading margins are long transform faults. These are where segments of the earth's crust grind past each other to cause earthquakes, like those on the San Andreas fault system in the USA.

The action of spreading ridges, trenches and transform faults breaks the earth's crust into plates.

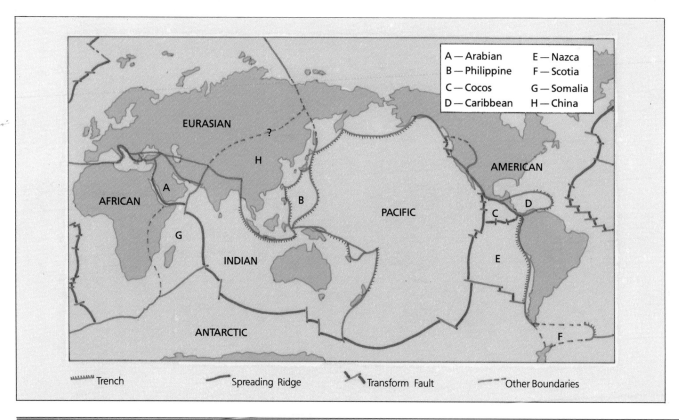

For at least the past 550 million years entire continents have been split apart and re-formed by the process of plate tectonics. Mantle plumes have linked to form spreading plate margins and continental collisions have welded plates together by forming mountain ranges.

Left A sulphide spring (fumarole) spurts iron and copper oxide from a crack in the ocean floor.

Below A constructive plate margin. Magma rises up to form volcanoes on the surface. As it cools it is magnetized by the earth's magnetic field at that time. Research has shown this magnetism to be regularly reversed, proving that the magnetic poles have changed places through earth history.

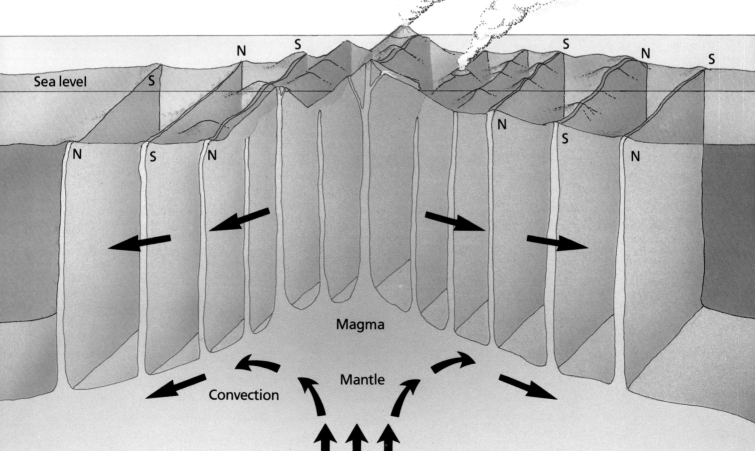

Sea level

N S S N S N S

N S N N S N

Magma

Mantle

Convection

Colliding plate margins

There are two types of plate collision, oceanic-continental collision, and continental – continental collision.

When an oceanic plate collides with a continental plate, the oceanic one dives beneath the continent along a plane called a Benioff zone. This creates a deep submarine trench. As it descends, the oceanic plate scrapes against the overlying plate to cause earthquakes. The intense pressure of the collision melts rock in the Benioff zone to produce magma. This magma then rises through the continental plate to form chains of coastal volcanoes, like the Andes of South America and the Cascades of North America.

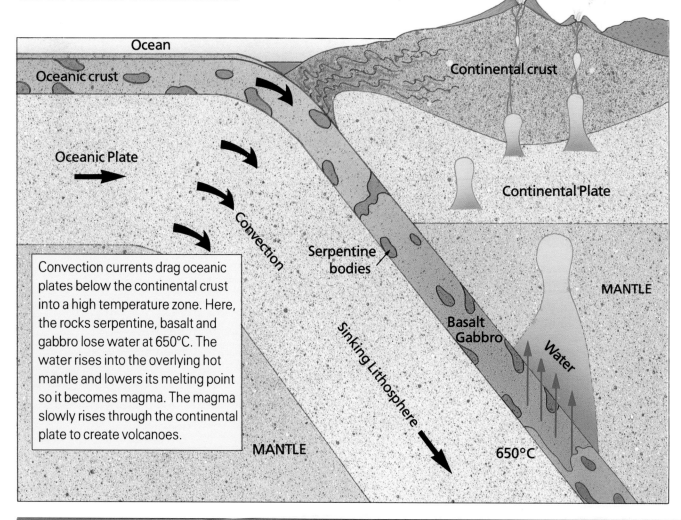

Ocean

Oceanic crust

Oceanic Plate

Continental crust

Continental Plate

Convection

Serpentine bodies

MANTLE

Convection currents drag oceanic plates below the continental crust into a high temperature zone. Here, the rocks serpentine, basalt and gabbro lose water at 650°C. The water rises into the overlying hot mantle and lowers its melting point so it becomes magma. The magma slowly rises through the continental plate to create volcanoes.

Sinking Lithosphere

Basalt Gabbro

Water

MANTLE

650°C

Continental–continental collision zones are marked by mountain ranges such as the Himalayas.

Island arcs take the place of continental margin volcanoes in many parts of the world. Island arcs are long, narrow volcanic islands bordering deep ocean trenches where oceanic crust is being destroyed. This generates earthquakes and causes volcanism, as is the case in Indonesia, the Aleutian Islands, the Philippines, Japan and the Kurile Isles. Some of the most disastrous eruptions known have been produced by volcanoes on these arcs, such as Krakatoa in Indonesia in 1883, and Mount Pelée in the Caribbean, in 1902.

Mountain chains are formed when two continents collide. As the continents are slowly pushed together by plate tectonics, part of the ocean floor between them is carried to destruction in deep trenches. Rock debris eroded from these colliding continents pours into the trenches where the oceanic plate is being destroyed. This adds to the ocean floor material to form thick sediments. When the two continents eventually meet, the sediments are folded and squeezed up, like putty in a vice. This creates mountains, such as the Alps and the Himalayas. The formation of these mountains welds the two continents together.

Mountains formed in this way always contain marine fossils, which is one of the clues that enable scientists to identify ancient plate collisions. The Urals in western USSR and the Appalachians in eastern USA mark the sites of continental collisions which took place over 250 million years ago. At that time, Europe became welded to Asia, New England to America, and Scotland and northern Ireland to England and southern Ireland.

Passive plate margins and hot-spots

Passive plate margins are not really passive at all, for they are nearly always on the move. They are called passive because they neither create new land, or destroy it. They occur where plates slide sideways against each other along transform faults. Transform faults are created when constructive plate margins are producing new crust along their length at different rates. Because movement along transform faults is not continuous, the plates bordering them stick, then move suddenly to produce shallow focus earthquakes.

The sudden movement along such faults caused the terrible earthquakes that destroyed Lisbon, Portugal, in 1775, and San Francisco, USA, in 1906.

The San Andreas Fault in California is really a combination of faults. These include a large transform fault with its southern end almost lost in a mass of smaller faults that carve the ground into large blocks. The San Andreas Fault was formed when part of the still active East Pacific Rise pushed itself under the American continental plate. This means that a splinter of the Californian coast is constantly trying to move to the north-west as part of the buried East Pacific Rise forms new crust. When the fault does move, earthquakes are generated, firstly by movement along the main fault, and secondly by movement along the smaller faults. This secondary movement happens as the blocks of crust disturbed by the first movement try to re-settle into position.

Hot-spots, or mantle plumes, were believed once to form deep inside the earth's mantle. Recent geological research, however, has shown they probably form at a much shallower level in the more plastic asthenosphere. This layer, thought to be close to its melting point, is where the slow circulations take place that carry the crustal plates on their journey around the planet.

Left A lava lake during the 1959 eruption of Kilauea, Hawaii, shows molten rock glowing through cracks in the cooled surface crust. Red-hot lava coats the far wall after a small explosion on the surface.

Opposite page Gas heaves globs of molten lava from the surface of a lava lake during the 1972 eruption of Mauna Ulu, Hawaii. The surface of the early earth must have resembled this.

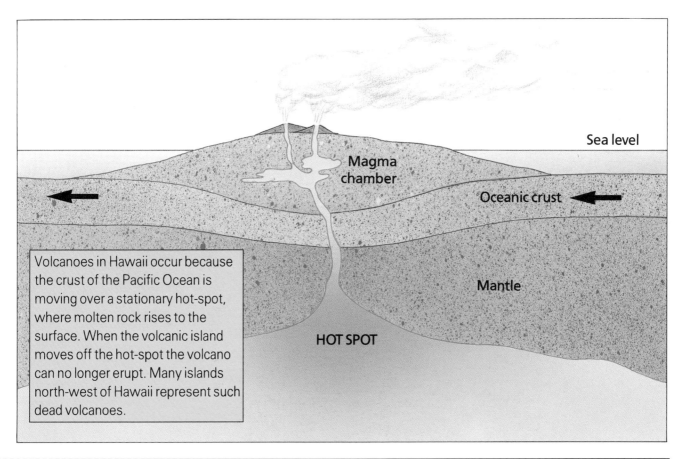

Sea level

Magma chamber

Oceanic crust

Mantle

HOT SPOT

Volcanoes in Hawaii occur because the crust of the Pacific Ocean is moving over a stationary hot-spot, where molten rock rises to the surface. When the volcanic island moves off the hot-spot the volcano can no longer erupt. Many islands north-west of Hawaii represent such dead volcanoes.

Types of volcano

There are three main types of volcanic eruption. These are Hawaiian, Strombolian and Plinian, and they give rise to nearly all volcanic forms known.

Hawaiian type eruptions produce spectacular fire fountains and release rivers of basalt lava that travel considerable distances. These eruptions are rarely violent or explosive, because basalt lava is fluid enough to allow the volcanic gases to escape easily and blow fragments of yellow-hot magma out of the volcano. The degassed lava then flows quietly from openings called boccas. Boccas are usually lower down the side of the volcano, below the main vent. Hawaiian activity produces shield volcanoes with very wide cones built up of layer upon layer of lava and black ash. Their gentle slopes rise sometimes to considerable heights.

Strombolian eruptions are more violent, producing thicker lava than those of Hawaiian type. Many fire fountains from small parasitic cones on large volcanoes are of Strombolian type. Since they erupt only once, they are called monogenetic.

Above Strombolian type activity. Known as the lighthouse of the Mediterranean, Stromboli is seen erupting in 1982. The fire fountains drop red-hot cinder down the side of the cone.

Left Hawaiian type activity. The lava of Hawaiian volcanoes has a low viscosity. This allows it to flow as rivers of molten rock for long distances. The lava from this 1959 eruption of Kilauea Iki is called a rootless flow since it is formed by molten material falling from the fire fountain rather than flowing from an opening in the ground.

Live volcanic fields, like those of Mexico and northern New Zealand, are littered with dead, monogenetic ash cones. Strombolian fire fountains are usually about 100 m in height and the ash is deposited mainly near the vent.

Plinian eruptions are named after Pliny, the Roman who observed and wrote about the eruption of Mt Vesuvius, Italy, in AD 79. Plinian events are some of the most destructive types of eruptions known, hurling enormous volumes of pumice as high as 50 km into the atmosphere, from where it falls over very wide areas. Pumice falls are followed often by pyroclastic flows, where hot gas and pumice ash pour out of the vent. These flows rush across the landscape, burning and burying all in their path. Such flows form thick deposits many kilometres from the vent.

The largest eruptions of all produce no cone, since the volcanic products are spread over immense areas. Cones form only where ash piles up around the vent.

Above Nuée ardente forming on the summit of New Zealand's Ngauruhoe volcano in 1972. A small plinian type eruption cloud collapses during an explosive eruption to form a glowing cloud of red-hot gas and lava. Large plinian-type eruptions release huge volumes of magma so the top of the volcano often collapses to form a large circular crater called a caldera.

Right Las Canadas on the island of Tenerife, Spain, is up to 300 m deep and 17 km across.

Products of volcanoes

When volcanoes erupt, fragments of volcanic rocks are hurled out of the vent. These fragments form pyroclastic deposits and are of two main types.

Pyroclastic fall, or air-fall deposits, result when rock fragments which have been thrown into the air by a volcanic gas blast fall to the ground through the air.

Pyroclastic flow, also called ash-flow, or nuées ardentes deposits, are formed when rock fragments which have been suspended in a red-hot cloud of gas eventually settle.

Air-fall deposits fall in layers of pale coloured pumice, or dark basaltic ash. They show a gradual increase in thickness towards the vent, but have an average depth of 3 m. The layers are usually fine at the base, and coarser towards the top. Lumps of molten lava that build up closely around a vent in basaltic eruptions form narrow circles of rock called spatter-rings. Basaltic eruptions that take place in water produce wide ash rings around the vent.

Ash-flow deposits are unsorted and not in layers. They have no relationship with their source and they often collect in valleys to form deposits over 100 m thick. Since these flows are at extremely high temperatures, when they come to rest they may weld into solid rock. They can travel as far as 100 km from the vent.

Over a long period of time pyroclastic deposits become compacted into solid rocks called tuffs. Welded tuffs, or ignimbrites, contain distinctive thin black streaks of volcanic glass called fiamme.

When air-fall pumice deposits are covered by an ash-flow, this indicates a change in the style of the eruption towards the end of the event.

Lava flows on land produce aa or pahoehoe deposits. Aa deposits have a rough upper and lower surface, with a solid centre, while pahoehoe deposits have a twisted, ropy upper surface above a solid centre. Both types contain hollow cavities which are caused by gas trapped in the flow when it cooled. Underwater flows produce pillow lavas, but in spite of their descriptive name they look more like branching, intertwined spaghetti. These are enclosed in fragmented lava that slowly changes, to form a yellow rock called palagonite.

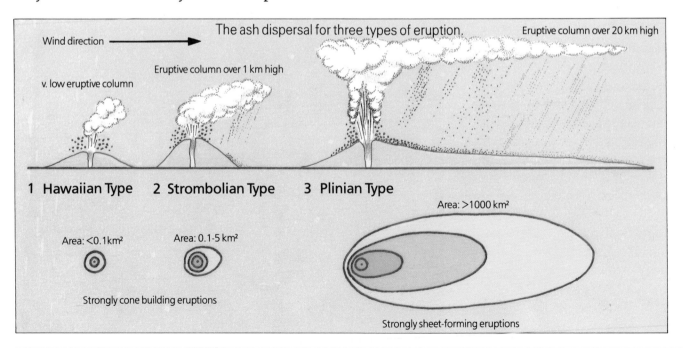

The ash dispersal for three types of eruption.

Wind direction

v. low eruptive column

Eruptive column over 1 km high

Eruptive column over 20 km high

1 Hawaiian Type   2 Strombolian Type   3 Plinian Type

Area: <0.1km²   Area: 0.1-5 km²   Area: >1000 km²

Strongly cone building eruptions

Strongly sheet-forming eruptions

Above Deposits of four eruptions in Tenerife, Spain.

Pahoehoe lava has a surface that looks like rope. The ropes are formed by small folds becoming wrapped in larger folds whilst the lava is molten.

A basalt dyke has cut through earlier ashes and an intrusive horizontal sill to feed a lava flow on the surface above in Tenerife, Spain.

Processes of volcanism

Volcanoes are like safety valves in the crust of the earth, releasing the massive pressure of gases that build up beneath it.

Under the high pressures that exist deep in the mantle, magma behaves like silicon rubber. It is elastic, plastic, brittle and ductile. Where these high pressures are reduced, the magma expands, becomes less dense and rises towards the surface. The gases dissolved in the magma begin to act as a flux as it nears the surface, allowing it to flow more easily. As long as the pressure of the overlying rock is greater than the gas pressure, an eruption will not take place.

When the gas pressure exceeds that of the overlying rock, the magma begins to degas, as when a bottle of Coca-Cola is opened. This suddenly releases high pressure gases that blast their way to the surface, causing an eruption.

Magma poor in silica, but rich in iron and magnesium, has a low viscosity, which means it is thin and runny. This allows gases to escape easily in spectacular fire fountains. The degassed magma

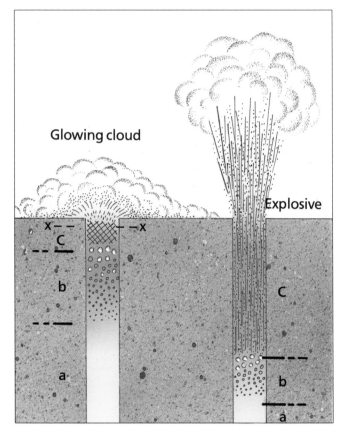

Glowing cloud

Explosive

Above In very viscous magma, gases cannot escape until they are near the top of the pipe (at **x——x**). This causes glowing clouds to form. Less viscous magma allows gases to escape more easily and blast rock fragments out of the pipe, like a giant shotgun. **a**–gaseous magma. **b**–magma with gas bubbles. **c**–gas dissolved in magma.

Left Nuées ardentes (glowing clouds) descend the slopes of Mayon volcano, in the Philippines, while a thick ash plume rises from the summit.

flows as lava from openings lower down the volcano. Magma rich in silica, but poor in iron and magnesium, has a high viscosity; it is thick and pasty. This prevents gases from escaping which causes high pressures to build up. Eventually the gases are released with explosive violence.

Eruptions end when there is no longer enough gas pressure to force magma to the surface. However, a falling gas pressure can dramatically change an eruption. If the gas pressure falls suddenly during a violent event, part of the eruption column is left without any support. Because of its immense weight it collapses around the vent to form glowing avalanches that rush outwards at speeds of over 120 kph. These flows also occur when a dense mixture of hot gas and dust pour out of the vent, like a fire-hydrant overflowing. The rock fragments in such flows are cushioned from each other by a coat of escaping hot gas. This keeps the flow mobile and prevents it from collapsing. It is only when the flow begins to cool that it finally comes to rest.

Fire fountains release gas and magma during the 1971 eruption of Mt Etna, in Italy.

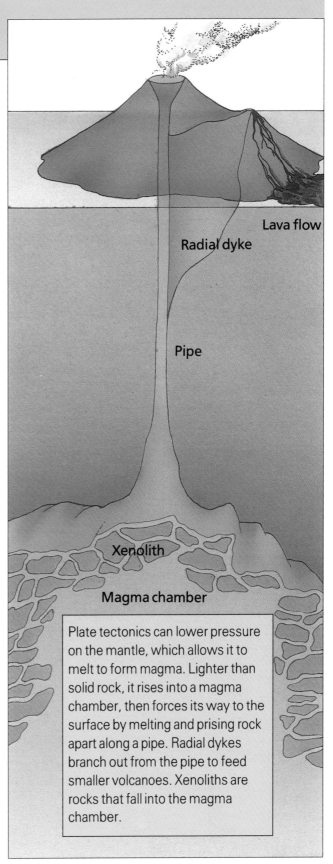

Lava flow

Radial dyke

Pipe

Xenolith

Magma chamber

Plate tectonics can lower pressure on the mantle, which allows it to melt to form magma. Lighter than solid rock, it rises into a magma chamber, then forces its way to the surface by melting and prising rock apart along a pipe. Radial dykes branch out from the pipe to feed smaller volcanoes. Xenoliths are rocks that fall into the magma chamber.

Fumaroles and hot springs

A fumarole is an opening in the ground in a volcanic area. Fumaroles release gases and steam. The gases carry elements which are dissolved in the vapours. As a result, the vent through which the gases flow is surrounded by mineral deposits. These are often brightly coloured and include carbonates, sulphates and chlorides of elements such as ammonia, sodium and iron. The deposits often contain small amounts of other elements such as zinc, copper, lead, manganese, cobalt and nickel.

The composition of fumarole gases give a helpful guide to the proportion of gases in magma. In Hawaii, calculations have shown the magma there contains less than 1 per cent of gas. This gas is made up of equal amounts of water (as steam), carbon dioxide and sulphurous acid. In addition, there are very small amounts of hydrochloric acid, hydrofluoric acid and carbon monoxide.

Above Sulphur crystals form on a fumarole.

Below Clad in an asbestos suit, a volcanologist measures gas speed from a fumarole on Mt Etna.

Algae and bacteria flourish in hot spring waters rich in chemicals in Yellowstone Park, USA.

Hot springs are similar to fumaroles, but contain a higher proportion of water to gases. Like fumaroles, hot springs occur mostly above buried masses of hot rock. Underground water, which circulates through cracks in the rock, comes into contact with this buried mass and is heated up. Once the water is hot, it rises to the surface and colder water sinks down to take its place.

Not all hot springs are connected with volcanoes. Some, like those at Larderello, in Italy, are due to water circulating deep enough in the crust to come into contact with the high temperatures that exist inside the earth.

Fumaroles and hot springs are found in active volcanic regions such as Yellowstone Park, in the USA, Wairakei in New Zealand and Solfatara, in Italy. They often occur inside volcanic craters, as at Vulcano, in Italy, as well as on the outer slopes of volcanoes. They also occur on lava fields and thick ash deposits. The fumaroles and hot springs on the thick ashes of Katmai, in Alaska, gave rise to the Valley of Ten Thousand Smokes. On Mt Erebus, in the Antarctic, steam from the fumaroles there has frozen around the vents to form ice chimneys over 20 m in height.

Geysers

Geysers are special kinds of hot springs that spout hot water and steam at regular intervals. They are named after the famous 'Great Geysir' of Iceland that was active for over 350 years. Its activity began to decrease in 1935 and today it can only be made to erupt by pouring soap down its throat. The soap reduces the surface tension of the water, which allows the steam to be released.

Geysers occur when ground water comes into contact with hot rock and heats up to as much as 150°C. Water usually boils at 100°C, but the pressure of the column of water in the geyser pipe prevents this superheated water from boiling. However, the water does expand and this causes the water in the pipe to overflow at the surface, so reducing the pressure. Eventually, a point is reached when the weight of the water column in the geyser pipe can no longer prevent the superheated water from boiling. When this happens, the water boils rapidly at an ever increasing speed until a large volume of it turns to steam, creating tremendous pressure. These high pressures blow the contents out of the geyser pipe as a spectacular fountain of steam and water. Once the pressure has been released the pipe refills with water and the process starts over again.

The time between each eruption varies from one geyser to the next. This is probably due firstly to the amount of water ejected by the previous eruption and secondly to the time taken for the system to refill and heat up to eruption point. Geyser vents usually occur on low mounds of pale coloured sinter, which is a porous quartz rock deposited from the water when it cools.

Yellowstone Park, in the USA, contains the world's greatest concentration of geysers and hot springs, with over 2,500 being active. Geysers die when their water feeder channels become blocked by clogging or earthquake movements. In 1959 a quake caused the death of several geysers in Yellowstone Park, yet at the same time it created new ones.

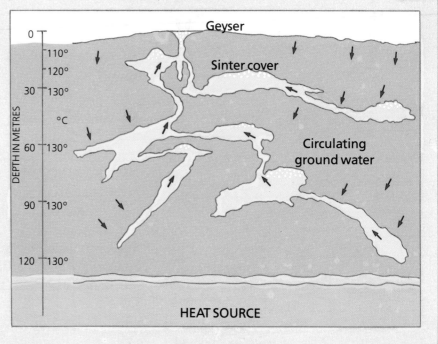

This diagram shows how geysers occur. Ground water circulating through porous rocks enters the cavities below the geyser. Rising heat provides the energy to drive the geyser system and raise the water to above its boiling point. The superheated water expands and overflows at the surface, thus reducing the pressure. This allows remaining water to flash into steam and cause an eruption. Hot water dissolves silica from the surrounding rocks and deposits it as sinter around the geyser.

Old Faithful geyser in Yellowstone Park, USA.
Inset Sinter deposited from Castle geyser has formed into terraces.

Geothermal energy

Geothermal energy is one of the most important resources of volcanic areas. Since historic times, people have used natural hot water to bath, wash and cook.

Many areas of hot ground that lie above magma chambers are able to provide a valuable and continuous source of geothermal energy. To do this, boreholes are sunk deep into the hot ground. Then, water is pumped into them. This is turned to steam by the heat, and the steam rushes to the surface and is used to drive the turbines that generate electricity.

The idea of using geothermal steam to generate electricity began at Larderello, in Italy, where metal cased boreholes were driven deep into the naturally hot ground. The high pressure steam for these wells was used to drive turbines to generate 300 million kilowatts of electricity each year. However, the acid gases in the steam soon began to damage the delicate machinery. The problem was solved by using the acid steam to heat acid-free water. This provided clean steam that would not damage the machinery. As a bonus, useful by-products were extracted from the acid steam, including boric acid,

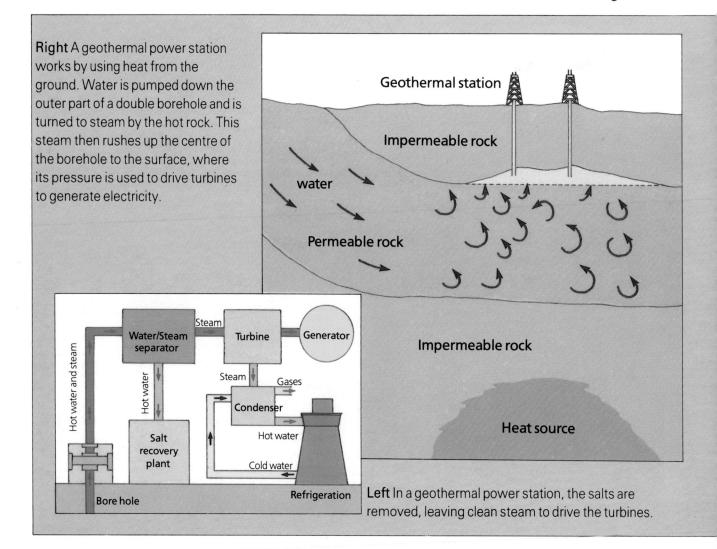

Right A geothermal power station works by using heat from the ground. Water is pumped down the outer part of a double borehole and is turned to steam by the hot rock. This steam then rushes up the centre of the borehole to the surface, where its pressure is used to drive turbines to generate electricity.

Geothermal station

Impermeable rock

water

Permeable rock

Impermeable rock

Heat source

Hot water and steam

Water/Steam separator

Steam

Turbine

Generator

Hot water

Steam

Gases

Condenser

Salt recovery plant

Hot water

Cold water

Bore hole

Refrigeration

Left In a geothermal power station, the salts are removed, leaving clean steam to drive the turbines.

ammonia and carbon dioxide.

In Reykjavik, the capital of Iceland, most of the homes are heated by hot water which is piped from underground heat sources. As a result, the city is almost free from air pollution. Outdoor swimming pools and glasshouse crops are heated throughout the winter, while electric turbines generate some 15,000 kilowatts per year. This is enough to run 5,000 electric heaters for a year at full power.

Geothermal plants in other volcanic areas include Geysers, which is outside San Francisco in the USA. This plant generates 13,000 kilowatts per year. The Wairakei geothermal station in New Zealand produces over 200,000 kilowatts of electricity per year, while the countries of Japan, Mexico and Chile operate similar, though smaller geothermal power stations.

Volcanoes themselves contain vast energy resources that could be used to provide unlimited supplies of electricity in the future. The problem of how to tap these endless energy supplies is still waiting to be solved.

Steaming well heads and pipelines of Wairakei geothermal power station in New Zealand.

Other resources

In prehistoric times man used a natural volcanic glass called obsidian to make sharp tools, such as knives and arrow heads. Obsidian was so valuable to prehistoric culture that ancient trade routes across Europe and Central America can be traced from the scattered pieces of this volcanic glass. It is still used today to make carved ornaments and figures for sale to tourists in Mexico.

Today, volcanic products are made from pumice, lava and ignimbrite. Finely powdered pumice is used in some toothpastes, cosmetics and abrasive cleaners. In its coarser state, pumice is spread on fields in hot countries to prevent water loss from the soil and to trap dew at night.

Lava is crushed, sieved and mixed with tar to provide roadsurfacing material. Ignimbrite can be sawn easily into blocks for building purposes. Many of the buildings in Cuzco, in Peru, and Naples, in Italy, are built from ignimbrite.

The formation of valuable ore and mineral deposits is closely linked with buried magma. Sometimes the magma itself contains the valuable ore, but it is mostly the rocks just above the magma chamber that are rich in these deposits. This happens because fluids, which are rich in elements from the magma, rise into the cracks and fissures that form above magma bodies.

Most of the world's copper and sulphur is mined from volcanic rocks. This includes the highest mine in the world, at Chuquicamata, in Chile, where sulphur is mined. Silver and gold were mined from volcanic deposits in the USA during the nineteenth century and the rich Bolivian deposit at Potosi, though mostly exhausted, is still in operation. In South Africa, the ancient volcanic pipes that contain kimberlite, a variety of the volcanic rock peridotite, are famous for having yielded some of the world's largest diamonds.

Above An ignimbrite building block being finished by a Mexican quarry worker at Guadalajara.

Right Gold is one of the precious metals that is concentrated by volcanic processes.

Left A farmer earths up potatoes grown in rich volcanic soil on a hillside terrace in Tenerife, Spain.

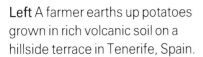

Earthquake hazards

Earthquakes present direct or indirect hazards. Direct hazards are due to the earthquake itself. Indirect hazards are events which are triggered by an earthquake.

During an earthquake, the severe ground vibrations make it difficult for people to stand. Everything shakes violently, poorly designed buildings crumble, windows break, trees are broken and church bells ring. Violent earthquakes destroy buildings of all types, railway lines are bent, large cracks open in the ground, dams and reservoirs burst and floods sweep through valleys, causing destruction and death.

The most disastrous indirect hazard is the tsunami, which is caused by an earthquake on the ocean floor. These waves often pass unnoticed at sea as extra large waves, but close to land, where the water is shallow, their height can increase dramatically to over 30 m. It was such killer waves that were responsible for the large death toll in Indonesia during the 1883 eruption of Krakatoa.

Other indirect hazards include mudflows and avalanches. In 1971 the earthquake that shook Yungay village, in Peru, caused a large piece of a glacier to break off Mt Huascaran. It swept down gorges, crashing from side to side, and within minutes had developed into a huge mudflow 80 m high. The mudflow swept through Yungay and its neighbouring villages, totally destroying them. It killed 50,000 people and made a further 800,000 people homeless.

While earthquakes cannot be prevented yet, scientists in the USA have suggested that water should be pumped into dangerous faults to lubricate them. As a result, they would move gently all the time and not build up dangerous stresses. In some cities, earthquake-proof buildings are constructed on reinforced concrete rafts. During all but the worst quakes the raft floats on the moving ground, allowing the building to survive.

Fire rages in Los Angeles, USA, after a minor earthquake.

Bluebird, California, USA, after an earthquake that destroyed homes and caused the road to fall 15 m.

Disaster relief and evacuation plans begin on a global scale once a major earthquake has taken its huge toll of human life. Relief workers and vehicles are sent by wealthier countries to help local forces fight disease, transport victims to safety, provide tents, clothing and other essentials. Whilst disaster appeals are being set up, UNDRO (United Nations Disaster Relief Co-ordinator) can give an immediate $50,000 to help a stricken area, and extend emergency grants up to $600,000 a year.

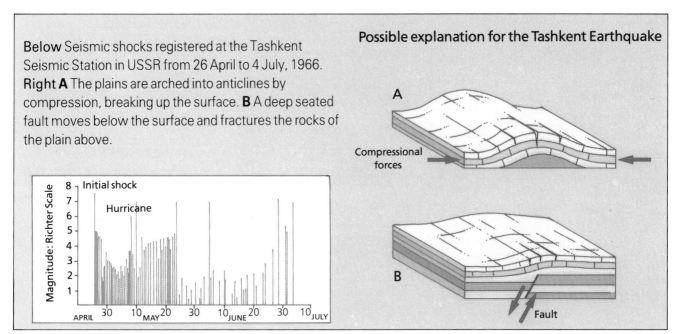

Below Seismic shocks registered at the Tashkent Seismic Station in USSR from 26 April to 4 July, 1966. **Right A** The plains are arched into anticlines by compression, breaking up the surface. **B** A deep seated fault moves below the surface and fractures the rocks of the plain above.

Possible explanation for the Tashkent Earthquake

A

Compressional forces

B

Fault

Predicting earthquakes

Earthquake prediction is a science that is still in its infancy, despite the research that is being carried out by seismologists throughout the world. China, Japan and the USA are ahead of other countries in making use of this new science.

Earthquakes can often be predicted, providing the technology is available. As with volcano prediction, it is the countries most at risk that cannot afford to maintain the costly equipment. Countries like the USA, where sufficient funds are available, have round-the-clock monitoring in sensitive areas such as California. Teams of scientists measure ground movements with a complex array of surveying instruments. The instruments, which include tiltmeters, creepmeters and mekometers, are linked by radio to monitoring stations by a process called telemetry. Other scientific instruments in use include magnetometers, gravimeters, resistivity gauges and scintillation counters.

The most valuable tool of all, however, is the seismogram. This is a very sensitive instrument that can detect small shocks deep below the surface. The movements are magnified and recorded on a slowly rotating drum to give a visual record of ground movements. This record is called a seismograph.

Since earthquakes are caused by the sudden release of stress that builds up in rocks, any method that detects this build up is valuable. All these complex and expensive instruments keep a check on any changes that are taking place in the rock layers underground.

Less scientific methods, such as watching the behaviour of animals, have given some surprising results. The Chinese found that certain animals leave an area shortly before an earthquake, while others are restless. As a result of such work, a city in China was evacuated in 1976, hours before an earthquake reduced it to ruins. However, a few years later another quake was not predicted, with disastrous results.

Even seismographs were unable to predict the quake that struck Mexico City in 1985, despite the fact that Mexico lies in a high technology continent. Surveillance of this kind, however unpredictable it may be, requires expensive equipment and skilled seismologists. The equipment is totally useless unless there are also skilled people to interpret the results.

Left The seismogram is made up of a sensor (left) which detects very small vibrations in the ground and converts them into an electrical current. This current passes to a drum recorder which amplifies the small signals and traces them on a chart (seismograph). The seismogram is often placed in remote areas where daily readings are not possible and is connected to a transmitter that relays the information to a central station.

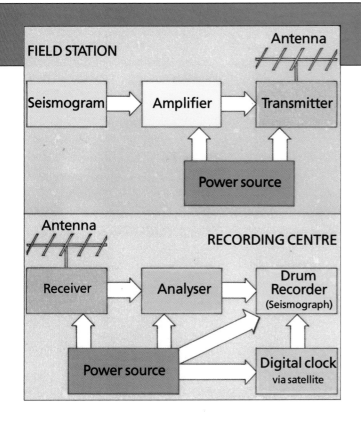

FIELD STATION

| Seismogram | → | Amplifier | → | Transmitter |

Antenna

Power source

RECORDING CENTRE

Antenna

| Receiver | → | Analyser | → | Drum Recorder (Seismograph) |

Power source

Digital clock via satellite

Left Monitoring earthquakes by telemetry. Since the field station may not be accessible on a daily basis the seismogram signals are fed into an amplifier and then a transmitter. The signals are then beamed via satellite to a central monitoring station. The field station is often powered by solar cells that use sunlight to generate electricity. A receiver picks up the signals bounced off the satellite and passes them to an analyzer, where the different earthquake waves are separated, before being traced on a large drum recorder.

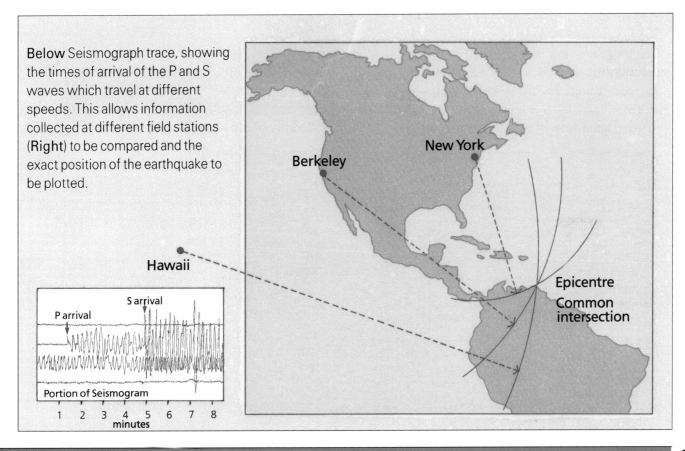

Below Seismograph trace, showing the times of arrival of the P and S waves which travel at different speeds. This allows information collected at different field stations (**Right**) to be compared and the exact position of the earthquake to be plotted.

Hawaii

Berkeley

New York

Epicentre
Common intersection

S arrival

P arrival

Portion of Seismogram

1　2　3　4　5　6　7　8
minutes

Volcanic hazards

There are two types of volcanic hazard: short term and long term hazards. Short term volcanic hazards occur several times every century, as the people living in Fornazzo and Mascalli, in Sicily, know well. Both these villages were threatened by lava flows in 1928, 1971 and 1979. Long term volcanic hazards occur less than once every hundred years, so most people living in volcanic areas are unlikely to experience them in their lifetime.

Direct volcanic hazards are caused by ash falls, ash flows, nuées ardentes, mudflows and lava flows. Indirect hazards include tsunamis, which are due to parts or products of volcanoes suddenly entering the sea.

Ash falls cause damage and injury by their fragments falling on people and property. During big eruptions entire towns may be buried, as was the case with Vestmannajyer, in Iceland, during the 1971 eruption.

Ash flows are very dangerous, high temperature flows that can devastate an area half the size of California. Travelling at speeds up to 350 kph, they can cross mountain barriers, as was the case with the prehistoric Ito flow, in Japan. This flow

Above During plinian eruptions a lava spine may be extruded and block the vent, allowing gases to build up to dangerously high pressures inside the volcano. Here, at Tequila volcano, Mexico, the gas pressures were too low to blow out the volcano top in a violently explosive eruption.

Left A lava flow buries a home on Heimaey during the eruption of Eldjfell volcano, Iceland, in 1973.

Left Houses being engulfed by a thick lava flow during the Eldjfell eruption.

Below Dead volcanoes are represented by old eroded spines in the Iran desert. These volcanoes will never erupt again and are quite safe.

travelled 70 km and crossed mountains 750 m high. The 1902 nuée ardente of Mt Pelée, in the Caribbean, travelled at 110 kph at temperatures high enough to cremate many of the 30,000 people caught in it.

When ash flows encounter water, such as a lake or torrential rain, they turn into mud flows, or lahars. An eruption in a crater lake can release lahars that cause immense damage. On Christmas Eve in 1953, an eruption of Mt Ruapehu, in New Zealand, melted the ice-blocked exit of a crater lake. This released a huge lahar that destroyed the Tangiwai bridge, five minutes before the Christmas Eve express was due. 151 people died when the train plunged into the torrent.

Lava flows are less destructive to human life because of their slow movement. Although their path can be predicted since they flow along valleys, they cause immense damage to property. Agricultural land on the island of Hawaii is regularly destroyed by lava flows. The 1783 eruption of Lakagigar fissure, in Iceland, produced lava flows that covered some 565 sq km of countryside. The lava flow released poisonous gases that killed more than half of the livestock and caused a famine in which 10,000 people died.

Predicting volcanoes

Three methods are used to predict volcanic eruptions. These include geophysical techniques, chemical techniques, and tephrochronology.

Geophysical methods measure any changes that occur in rocks below the surface. As magma rises, it forces rocks apart, which creates swarms of tiny earthquakes that can be detected with seismographs. A comparison of three or more seismograms enables scientists to pin-point exactly where magma is splitting rocks during its rise to the surface. This technique is so successful that in Hawaii the place and time of eruptions have been forecasted accurately. Before an eruption, many volcanoes swell as magma rises into them. This causes the ground to tilt. The tilt can be measured with tiltmeters and surveying instruments.

Movement of magma at depth also causes gravity changes. These changes can be detected with gravimeters. Also, when rock rises above a certain temperature it loses its magnetism, which is measured with magnetometers. Another prediction method uses infra-red temperature surveys. These show which parts of a volcano are heating up, as magma rises near the surface.

Chemical methods are used to determine the volcanic gases at fumaroles and hot springs. Just before an eruption, an increase occurs in chlorine compounds, sulphur oxides, carbon dioxide, hydrogen and radon.

Tephrochronology is a method which relies on the careful mapping of volcanic ashes to discover what type of eruptions have occurred in the past. It can also determine how big the eruptions were, how long they lasted and what areas they affected. Rest periods between eruptions can be worked out by atomic age dating, which enables volcanologists to estimate how frequently a volcano erupts.

Once an eruption begins, the people living near the volcano are evacuated. Sometimes entire towns are evacuated at great expense, on the advice of officials or scientists who have no knowledge of volcanology at all. One report suggests that the population of St Pierre on Martinique, in the Caribbean, were prevented from leaving in 1902 because politicians there wanted the largest possible turn-out for an election. More than 30,000 people died a few days later when the city was wiped out.

Anemometer funnel and thermocouple probes on a jig. All parts are of stainless steel to resist high temperature corrosion. The funnel contains vanes that revolve in gas jets and measure the gas speed, while the thermocouple measures the gas temperature. Even the stainless steel did not stand up to the corrosive acid gases and the anemometer funnel and vanes had to be renewed after each measurement.

Above Officials discussing how to divert a huge lava flow to prevent Fornazzo village being destroyed during the eruption of Mt Etna in 1971. The lava actually diverted itself by flowing into a gorge alongside the village.

Right When a magma chamber fills with fresh molten rock it causes the cone to swell. This swelling is greatest when magma is just beneath the surface and can be measured with tiltmeters to discover where the eruption is going to occur. The tiltmeter record shows that the swelling subsides after each eruption.

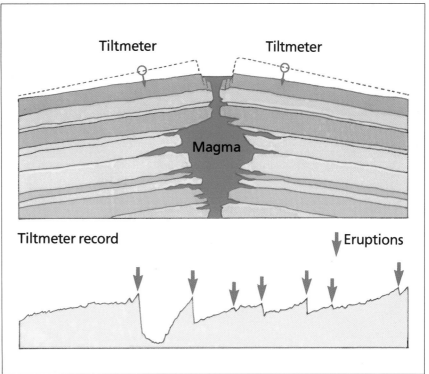

Tiltmeter   Tiltmeter

Magma

Tiltmeter record   ↓ Eruptions

Glossary

Aa lava A lava flow with a rough surface covered with coky fragments.

Ash fall A product of a volcanic eruption where rock blasted out of the vent falls over the land like snow.

Ash-flow A volcanic product where pumice and rock dust is carried along while supported by hot gases.

Asthenosphere The layer of rocks beneath the surface of the earth that is able to flow and carry the continental plates around the surface of our planet.

Basalt A volcanic rock with a high proportion of iron and magnesium, formed by rapid cooling.

Benioff zone A steeply dipping zone where an oceanic plate is carried below a continental plate.

Bocca The opening through which magma reaches the surface to form lava flows.

Caldera A large hollow formed by the upper part of a volcano collapsing into its own magma chamber.

Chemical prediction A method of predicting eruptions which relies upon changes in volcanic gases.

Continental collision The meeting of two moving continental plates during continental drift, resulting in the formation of mountain ranges.

Continental volcano A volcano that forms on a continental plate, as opposed to an oceanic one.

Creepmeter An instrument used for measuring the speed at which rocks move past each other.

Dense Rock that is very heavy for its volume.

Dormant volcano A volcano that is live and likely to erupt again but shows no sign of activity at the present.

Ductile Material that can be stretched without breaking.

Elastic Material that can be stretched but returns to its original form afterwards.

Element A single substance, like iron, that cannot be broken down further by a chemical process.

Epicentre The point on the earth's surface above the focus of an earthquake.

Fiamme Dark, usually black, streaks of volcanic glass found in ignimbrites.

Fire fountain A very hot gas blast that throws out molten rock.

Fissure A long crack, or fault, through which gas and magma finds its way to the earth's surface.

Flux A chemical that lowers the melting point of a solid.

Focus A point or place where rocks fracture to produce an earthquake.

Fumarole An opening in the ground from which gases escape.

Geophysical prediction A method for predicting earthquakes and volcanic eruptions that measures the physical properties of rocks.

Geothermal energy Energy obtained from hot zones deep below the surface of the earth.

Gravimeter An instrument that measures gravity.

Hawaiian eruption An eruption of thin runny lava from which gases can escape easily.

Hot-spot A place on the surface of the earth beneath which hot rock is rising to the surface.

Ignimbrite Volcanic rock that results from the collapse of a glowing avalanche cloud.

Island arc A long curved volcanic island or chain of islands produced above a destructive plate margin.

Kimberlite A rock which cooled under very high pressures, resulting in the formation of crystalline carbon (diamond).

Lahar A mudflow, which can be either cold or very hot.

Lava Molten rock that flows at the earth's surface.

Magma Molten rock beneath the earth's surface.

Magma chamber A cavity, or series of tubes and fissures in which magma collects.

Magnetic field The space around a magnet within which magnetic forces are exerted.

Magnetometer An instrument that measures the variation in the earth's magnetic field at any point.

Mantle The part of the earth that lies between the surface crust and the core, at the centre.

Mantle plume Molten rock which is rising to the surface.

Mekometer A very accurate instrument that uses a laser beam to measure distance.

Monogenetic volcano A volcano that erupts only once.

Nuée ardente   A red-hot cloud of gas and volcanic ash.

Obsidian   Volcanic glass, similar in composition to granite.

Oceanic volcano   A volcano that forms on an oceanic plate.

Pahoehoe lava   The Hawaiian term for ropy lava.

Palagonite   A yellow mineral that gives its name to altered, fragmented pillow lavas.

Parasitic cone   A small cone on the side of a large volcano.

Passive plate margin   Transform fault.

Peridotite   Rock from the region of the mantle that is composed mostly of the mineral olivine.

Pillow lava   Lava that has formed under water.

Plastic   Able to be shaped and to remain in any form.

Plate   One of several large fragments that make up the surface of the earth.

Plate boundary   See plate margin.

Plate margin   The edge of a plate.

Plate tectonics   The theory which explains how the continents and oceans have formed, been destroyed and reformed over geological time.

Plinian eruption   An eruption of great violence which throws fragmented rock as high as 50 km.

Polygenetic volcano   A large volcano that erupts from time to time over thousands of years.

Pumice   Highly porous rock that contains the remains of gas cavities.

Pyroclastic deposit   A deposit of fragmented (clastic) rocks formed at high temperature (pyro).

Pyroclastic fall   The fall of pyroclastic rocks from an eruption.

Pyroclastic flow   See nuée ardente.

Resistivity gauge   An electrical instrument which measures the resistance of rock to electricity.

Richter Scale   A mathematical scale that is used to represent the scale or size of an earthquake.

Scintillation counter   An instrument used to detect radioactivity.

Sediments   Rock debris deposited by ice, water or gas.

Seismogram   An instrument that detects earthquakes.

Seismograph   A graph that is traced on the seismogram.

Seismologist   A scientist who studies earthquakes.

Shield volcano   A polygenetic volcano with a gentle slope, composed of thin layers of lava and volcanic ash.

Silica   Silicon dioxide or glass.

Silicon rubber   A synthetic substance that resembles natural magma.

Sinter   Coky, porous quartz deposited by hot water around springs and geysers.

Spatter ring   A ring of lava formed around a vent.

Spreading plate margin   A series of long fissures in a submarine rift valley up which magma flows to the surface.

Stress   Energy that is created when two forces work against each other.

Strombolian eruption   An eruption in which the magma is thick and from which gas cannot escape easily.

Superheated   Heated above boiling point.

Surface tension   The physical property due to the molecular structure of a surface. In the case of water it allows small insects to walk on it.

Telemetry   The transfer of data by satellite from instruments in remote places to a central processing unit.

Tephrochronology   The study of volcanic ash and rock to learn about their order of formation and history.

Tiltmeter   An instrument that measures the tilt that occurs when volcanoes swell as magma rises into them.

Transform fault   A fault that forms in response to uneven generation of new crust at constructive plate boundaries. Also known as passive plate margins.

Tsunami   A giant sea wave caused by an earthquake.

Tuff   Volcanic ashes that have become compacted over geological time.

Volcanic pipe   The tube that connects the opening at the top of a volcano with its magma chamber below.

Viscosity   A measure of how fluid a liquid is.

Welded tuff   Volcanic rocks produced from the nuées ardentes that have become compacted into rock through the passage of time.

Further reading

Booth, Basil and Fitch, Frank, *Earthshock* (J.M. Dent, 1979)

Carson, James, *Volcanoes* (Wayland, 1983)

Dudman, John, *The San Francisco Earthquake* (Wayland, 1988)

Fifield, R., *The Making of the Earth* (Basil Blackwell and New Scientist, 1985)

Francis, P., *Volcanoes* (Penguin Books, 1976)

The Geological Museum *Earthquakes* (H.M.S.O., 1974)

The Geological Museum *Volcanoes* (H.M.S.O., 1974)

Jollands, David (ed.), *Earth, Sea and Sky* (Cambridge University Press, 1984)

Macdonald, G.A., *Volcanoes* (Prentice-Hall, 1972)

Matthews, Rupert, *The Eruption of Krakatoa* (Wayland, 1988)

Rittman, A. & L., *Volcanoes* (Orbis, 1976)

Rosen, Mike, *The Destruction of Pompeii* (Wayland, 1987)

Tazieff, Haroun, and Sabroux, J.C., *Forecasting Volcanic Events* (Elsevier, 1983)

Tazieff, Haroun, *Nyiragongo, the Forbidden Volcano* (Cassell, 1975)

Walker, Bryce, *Planet Earth: Earthquake* (True Life Books, 1982)

Picture acknowledgements

The publishers would like to thank the following for allowing their photographs to be reproduced in this book: BBC Hulton Picture Library 9, 10, 11; Bruce Coleman Ltd *front cover, main picture*; TOPHAM 36, 37; Wayland *back cover*; ZEFA *front cover, inset*; all other photographs with special thanks to GeoScience Features Library. All illustrations by Malcolm Walker.

Index